LITTLE MONSTER'S ALPHABET BOOK

by Mercer Mayer

to Anne

go Golden Press · New York

Western Publishing Company, Inc.
Racine, Wisconsin

Library of Congress Catalog Card Number: 77-90978

ISBN 0-307-11847-9

I have an alphabet collection. There is something in it for every letter of the alphabet.

Aa is a brown, grumpy apple that's been on the ground all winter.

Bb is a balloon I collected from Dr. Windbag on my last visit.

Cc

Cc is for color. I collect something for every color in the rainbow.
You can remember all the colors of the rainbow by making a name out of them:

R **O** **Y** **G.** **B** **I** **V.**
E **R** **E** **R** **L** **N** **I**
D **A** **L** **E** **U** **D** **O**
  N **L** **E** **E** **I** **L**
  G **O** **N** **G** **E**
  E **W**   **O** **T**

YELLOW hat

ORANGE orange

VIOLET grapes

RED wagon

BLUE overalls

GREEN unripe bananas

INDIGO an Indigo Snake

Dd
is a dragon and they are much too big to collect so I collected a duck instead.

Ee is an egg I just collected.
Oops! Baby dragons come in eggs!

Ff

is a field of fireflies. I collect some
in a jar, but I let them go before I go inside.

Gg is for the games I like to play.

Hh is for helping.
How many ways can you help?

Ii

Ii is for insect. I have a pet ladybug and a cricket, but I don't want a pet spider.

Jj

Jj is a jester. I have a jester costume and I tell jokes. I also collect jelly beans and I eat them as fast as I can collect them.

Kk

is a key. I collect keys.

Ll

is the lock on my secret chest, but I have so many keys that I never can find the right one.

Mm is my magnet.
I collect things that stick to my magnet.

Nn is a nut.
Squirrels collect nuts
to store in their nests
for the winter.

Oo

Oo is for anything old. I have lots of old stuff in my collection. Right now I have my old overalls on because I'm painting a picture

Pp

old can

old shoe

old chair

old overalls

Sometimes I use a brush and sometimes I use my fingers. It's much more fun to use my fingers.

$\mathbf{Qq}$ is a question. I collect questions to ask my Grandpa.

Rr is my red rubber raft.

Ss is the sea,
a ship on the sea,
a snail and some shells on the beach.
I have five shells in the S-part of my alphabet collection.

Tt

is my collection of toys—my toy-trunk, top, train, truck, and tricycle.

Uu

is something useless. I can't think of anything to use it for, but it's real neat.

Vv is a visit from Grandma and Grandpa on Valentine's Day.
I collect visits on other days, too, like my birthday and Christmas.

Ww is collecting wheels in my wagon.

Xx is the skull and crossbones flag flying from my pirate ship.

Yy is my yellow yo-yo.

Zz

is my Zipperump-a-zoo. I take him to see all the other strange creatures in Professor Wormbog's Monster Zoo.

Why don't you start
your own alphabet collection?